WEEKLY WR READER
EARLY LEARNING LIBRARY

What Happens at a

Bakery?

¿Qué pasa en

una panadería?

Where People **Work**
¿Dónde **trabaja** la gente?

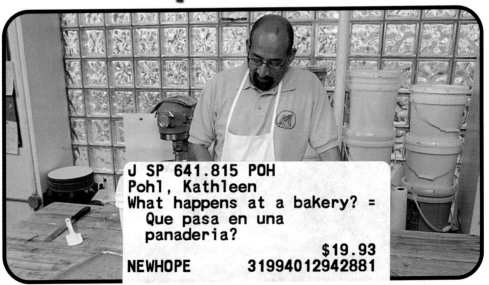

by/por Kathleen Pohl

Reading consultant/Consultora de lectura: Susan Nations, M.Ed., author, literacy coach,
consultant in literacy development/autora, tutora de alfabetización, consultora de desarrollo de la lectura

Please visit our web site at: www.garethstevens.com
For a free color catalog describing Weekly Reader® Early Learning Library's list
of high-quality books, call 1-877-445-5824 (USA) or 1-800-387-3178 (Canada).
Weekly Reader® Early Learning Library's fax: (414) 336-0164.

Library of Congress Cataloging-in-Publication Data

Pohl, Kathleen.
    [What happens at a bakery? Spanish & English]
    What happens at a bakery? = Qué pasa en una panadería? / Kathleen Pohl.
       p. cm. — (Where people work = Dónde trabaja la gente?)
    Includes bibliographical references and index.
    ISBN-10: 0-8368-7385-8 — ISBN-13: 978-0-8368-7385-6 (lib. bdg.)
    ISBN-10: 0-8368-7392-0 — ISBN-13: 978-0-8368-7392-4 (softcover)
    1. Baking—Vocational guidance—Juvenile literature. 2. Bakers—Juvenile literature.
  I. Weekly Reader Early Learning Library (Firm) II. Title. III. Title: Qué pasa en una panadería?
  IV. Series: Pohl, Kathleen. Where people work (Spanish & English)
    TX765.P6418   2007
    641.8'15023—dc22   2006016359

This edition first published in 2007 by
Weekly Reader® Early Learning Library
A Member of the WRC Media Family of Companies
330 West Olive Street, Suite 100
Milwaukee, Wisconsin 53212 USA

Copyright © 2007 by Weekly Reader® Early Learning Library

Buddy® is a registered trademark of Weekly Reader Corporation. Used under license.

Managing editor: Dorothy L. Gibbs
Art direction: Tammy West
Cover design and page layout: Scott M. Krall
Picture research: Diane Laska-Swanke and Kathleen Pohl
Photographer: Jack Long
Translation: Tatiana Acosta and Guillermo Gutiérrez

Acknowledgments: The publisher thanks Jorge Lopez, Luis Gutierrez, and Raquel delaCruz Gutierrez
for modeling in this book. Special thanks to Jorge Lopez, of Lopez Bakery, for his expert consulting
and the use of his bakery's facilities.

Printed in the United States of America

1 2 3 4 5 6 7 8 9 10 09 08 07 06

Hi, Kids!

I'm Buddy, your Weekly Reader® pal. Have you ever visited a bakery? I'm here to show and tell what happens at a bakery. So, come on. Turn the page and read along!

– – – – – – – –

¡Hola, chicos!

Soy Buddy, su amigo de Weekly Reader®. ¿Han estado alguna vez en una panadería? Estoy aquí para contarles lo que pasa en una panadería. Así que vengan conmigo. ¡Pasen la página y vamos a leer!

A bakery smells so good! It is full of yummy things to eat. People love to shop at a bakery.

— — — — — — — —

¡Qué bien huele una panadería! Y está llena de cosas deliciosas. A la gente le encanta comprar en una panadería.

Mr. Lopez is a baker. He bakes
bread and rolls. He bakes cakes
and cookies, too.

— — — — — — — — —

El señor López es panadero.
Hornea barras de pan y panecillos.
También hornea tartas y galletas.

Today, Mr. Lopez is going to make twenty cakes! One of them will be a birthday cake for Luis.

— — — — — — — —

¡Hoy, el señor López va a hacer veinte tartas! Una de ellas será la tarta de cumpleaños de Luis.

First, Mr. Lopez makes **batter**. He uses lots of flour and sugar and eggs. He mixes them all in a big **mixer**.

— — — — — — — —

Primero, el señor López prepara la **masa**. Usa un montón de harina y azúcar y huevos. Lo mezcla todo en una gran **amasadora**.

mixer/amasadora

Then he pours the batter into pans. He uses round pans and square pans and **sheet pans**.

— — — — — — — —

Después, echa la masa en moldes. Usa moldes redondos y moldes cuadrados y **bandejas de hornear**.

sheet pan/
bandeja de hornear

13

The cakes bake in a big **oven**. They are very hot when they come out. The baker puts them on a tall **rack** to cool.

– – – – – – – –

Las tartas se hornean en un gran **horno**. Cuando se sacan, están muy calientes. El panadero las pone a enfriar en un **carro bandejero**.

oven/horno

rack/carro bandejero

15

Now the cakes need frosting! Mr. Lopez **pipes** yellow frosting through the tip of a **frosting bag**. He makes a pretty border around Luis's cake.

– – – – – – – –

¡Ahora hay que decorar la tarta! El señor López echa crema amarilla con la punta de una **manga pastelera**. Hace un bonito borde alrededor de la tarta de Luis.

frosting bag/
manga pastelera

17

Next, he fills the bag with red frosting. He uses other colors, too. He makes pictures on cakes with frosting.

— — — — — — — —

Después, llena la manga con crema roja. También pone otros colores. El señor López usa la manga para hacer dibujos sobre las tartas.

Look at Luis's cake now!
Happy birthday, Luis.

— — — — — — — — —

¡Mira la tarta de Luis!
Luis, ¡feliz cumpleaños!

🐻 Glossary/Glosario

batter — a mixture of flour, sugar, eggs, water, and butter or oil that is thin enough to pour

border — a line or strip along the outside edge of something

frosting bag — a plastic bag with one corner cut off, where a special tip is attached for piping out frosting in different designs

pipes — pushes frosting out of a frosting bag to make a decorative pattern or design

sheet pans — large, flat baking pans for making big cakes that have only one layer

— — — — — — — —

bandejas de hornear — bandejas grandes y planas para hornear dulces grandes de una sola capa

borde — línea que rodea el límite exterior de algo

manga pastelera — bolsa con un extremo recortado en el que se inserta una punta especial para hacer diferentes diseños echando crema

masa — mezcla de harina, azúcar, huevos, agua y mantequilla o aceite que se puede echar en un recipiente

For More Information/Más información

Books/Libros

El autobús mágico dentro de un pastel: un libro sobre cocina.
Joanna Cole (Scholastic)

Jelly Beans from Start to Finish. Made in the USA (series).
Claire Kreger (Blackbirch Press)

La panadería. Lee y aprende (series).
Catherine Anderson (Heinemann)

Out and About at the Bakery. Jennifer A. Ericsson
(Picture Window Books)

¡Zas! Rookie español (series).
Mary Margaret Pérez-Mercado (Children's Press)

Index/Índice

About the Author

Kathleen Pohl has written and edited many children's books. Among them are animal tales, rhyming books, retold classics, and the forty-book series *Nature Close-Ups*. She also served for many years as top editor of *Taste of Home* and *Country Woman* magazines. She and her husband, Bruce, live among beautiful Wisconsin woods and share their home with six goats, a llama, and all kinds of wonderful woodland creatures.

- -

Información sobre la autora

Kathleen Pohl ha escrito y corregido muchos libros infantiles. Entre ellos hay cuentos de animales, libros de rimas, versiones nuevas de cuentos clásicos y la serie de cuarenta libros *Nature Close-Ups*. Además, trabajó durante muchos años como directora de las revistas *Taste of Home* y *Country Woman*. Kathleen vive con su marido, Bruce, en los bellos bosques de Wisconsin. Ambos comparten su hogar con seis cabras, una llama y todo tipo de maravillosos animales del bosque.